CYBERSECURITY
ON A BUDGET

Free and low-budget security tools to protect
against cyber-attacks

BY

DR. CYBERCARE

Table of Contents

Introduction

The security of data and assets is becoming more tasking as threats evolve. No wonder the cybersecurity budgets continue to reflect this complexity. There are indications from analyzed data that the spending on cybersecurity is outgrowing the aggregate expenditure on IT. Gartner's press release estimated about 10.5% spending on security in 2019 while IT spending saw a 0.4% growth in spending.

According to Enterprise Strategy Group, 62% of companies surveyed planned to step up their cybersecurity budget from 2020, while 36% planned to keep their budget flat. With the evolution of threats and the increasing need for organizations to be cyber-resilient, it is expedient for businesses to leverage free and open-source cybersecurity tools to keep up with their cybersecurity budget.

This book's essence is to unveil open source, free, and low budget tools to implement the basic critical security controls.

CHAPTER TWO

Free, Open-Source Cybersecurity Tools for Asset Inventory Management

It is paramount for organizations to acquire different hardware and software tools crucial for their daily operations' smooth running. It is also expedient to find possible means of managing asset inventory.

However, if you are running a small business, it is not profitable to acquire expensive tools to achieve this objective. You can leverage free and open-source software to manage your asset inventory.

Here are some of the tools:

AssetTiger

This is cloud-based software that allows you to track your check-ins and check-outs, as well as record how all your assets interact. The tool enables you to implement internal audits and set alarms not to miss crucial maintenance schedules. You can also manage your asset licenses and establish an alert system for their renewals.

Small businesses can leverage the free version, which supports about 250 assets.

ManageEngine AssetExplorer

This is a web application that automatically searches your network in a bid to discover both hardware and software assets and patches the inventory.

You can use the software's configuration management database to set up and keep an eye on how business-critical assets interact. It has a license and contract management feature. While the free version never expires and supports every available functionality, you can only use it on 25 workstations.

Snipe-IT

It is another open-source software that permits end-to-end monitoring of all assets- their history (check-ins, check-outs, as well as maintenance), their present status (pending, deployed, broken, archived, etc.), and their allocation (physical location or assignee). Not only that, but the tool also provides functionalities that support auditing of assets, digital signatures, reports, license management, alerts on licenses and warranties, integration with QR code readers, as well as barcode scanners.

The self-hosted plan is free and can take unlimited assets and users, coupled with Github community support.

Spice-works

This tool provides different types of IT management features coupled with a software inventory. It inventories both Windows and Mac computers and scans different devices using an agentless network device (without agent software installation). You can access the service either in the cloud or on-premises, though some functionality differences exist between these deployment procedures.

Lansweeper

It's a tool that employs both agent-based and agentless discovery. It can scan for different types of networks- Windows, Linux, as well as OSX devices. You can use the product for free on up to 100 devices.

Microsoft Map Toolkits

Windows Infrastructure Specialists employ Microsoft Assessment & Planning Toolkit in planning upgrades and migrations. However, MAP Toolkit remains an effective cross-platform inventory product capable of reporting on different software and computers. Its functionality is not limited to planning and managing Microsoft's software stack (SQL Server, Exchange, and HyperV), but it can also ingest data across different systems like VMWare. You need a Windows desktop or server to deploy MAP exclusively on-premise.

Now that you have different options to choose from, the next question on your mind is, 'Which of the free and open-source software should you choose? These steps will enable you to pick the best software that suits your business requirement.

- Create a poll within your team to share what they expect an ITAM software to have.
- Explore their issues and, based on that, pick tools that seek to solve those issues.
- Check Capterra for reviews to collate the first-hand experience about your choice.
- Assess the free offerings and factor in what it will cost to upgrade. Also, check for any hidden charges.

CHAPTER TWO

Continuous Vulnerability Management Tools On-Budget

Vulnerability Management Tools form a crucial component of any organization's security strategies. It's also a security best practice to scan applications for vulnerabilities. While most tools out there can be expensive, open-source vulnerability assessment tools can save you money and provide a solution that meets your need.

Here are some useful open-source vulnerability management tools you can leverage. These tools include web server and software vulnerability scanners, general vulnerability assessment tools, analysis tools, as well as fuzzers.

Nexpose Community

Rapid7 designed the Nexpose vulnerability tool with the capability to scan over 68,000 vulnerabilities and check over 163,000 networks. The community edition, restricted to 32 IP addresses and one user, can be accessed by Windows or Linux users for free. While it can't scan web applications, it has an automatic vulnerability update, as well as Microsoft-patch Tuesday vulnerability updates.

OpenVAS

It's another open-source vulnerability assessment manager. OpenVAS is a fork or a branch of the previous Nessus vulnerability scanner. The engine is updated with the latest network vulnerability tests daily (NVTs).

Clair

It's a dedicated container vulnerability solution that highlights different vulnerabilities that may endanger your container and alert you of the latest vulnerabilities that can threaten existing containers. The tool analyzes each container once without executing it to implement its examination. All required data are extracted to check for known vulnerabilities before caching later data for checks against subsequent vulnerabilities.

Powerfuzzer

Powerfuzzer is an automated and fully customizable HTTP protocol-based software fuzzer. It has the capability of discovering the following issues: injections (LDAP, SQL, commands, code, CRLF, and XPATH), HTTP 500 statuses (misconfiguration of security flaws, i;e buffer overflow), and cross-site scripting (XSS).

Moloch

A large scale, open-source IPv4 capturing, indexing, coupled with a database system which provides a web interface for packet capture browsing.

Qualys Community Edition

It is a free, cloud-based solution that replaced the former Qualys FreeScan tool suitable for small businesses. It comes with an unlimited scanning feature for sixteen internal assets, three external assets, and one website address. It includes all features present in the full package as it leverages data from over three billion scans completed each year. This scan engine can also generate reports from scan results. The user interface is attractive to use.

Burp Suite Community Edition

Enterprise and Professional level users can access the free version of this tool. Administrators who desire manual control can leverage Burp Suite web-based vulnerability scanning. They can manage prompts and responses, annotate a list of items and engage match-and-replace rules in applying custom changes. Burp is an effective and great free option if you want to build a tool for web scanning.

While you can't fix all vulnerabilities, you can manage them by tackling the ones that put your organization at the most significant risk. Here are some useful tips for managing exposures:

1. Ascertain your server software and workstation is updated.

Commodity malware takes advantage of vulnerabilities in servers and workstations. Patch those vulnerabilities to minimize the threat surface and reduce the occurrence of known vulnerabilities before scanning. Use free and open-source patch management tools such as Comodo One Windows Patch Management and Pulseway.

2. List and map all assets

You can only protect assets that you are aware of—inventory all assets, including your services, devices, open ports both in the cloud and on-premise. Figure out shadow IT infrastructures and delist unimportant, old gadgets and open ports. Network components such as applications, services, and devices are continually changing, so frequent inventory should be prioritized.

3. Scan vulnerabilities regularly

Perform vulnerability scanning regularly. A single scan is not enough as new vulnerabilities are unveiled every new day. You need to intensify scanning to stay updated with the current situation. It is also a great way to ensure previously discovered problems have been fixed. Also, ensure you scan hosted services by your vendors.

4. Prioritize the most significant vulnerabilities

Scanning ensures you can identify several vulnerabilities. While it reveals a lot of them, you cannot tackle them all. That is the more reason you need to focus on the most critical infrastructures. Based on the holistic asset inventory you have done, you can list these important assets and focus on them. Also, don't isolate a single asset; address their relationships with the entire network and the internet. Figure out the impact of an exploited vulnerability on the whole network and deal with the most severe vulnerabilities across all endpoints and services.

5. Keep a record of the scan results

Documenting scan results will enable you to track the changes you have made during the review.

6. Establish plans for unresolved vulnerabilities

Since you can't patch all vulnerabilities, it is expedient to establish a mitigation plan to reduce the likely exploitations of those vulnerabilities. Mark them as a known risk and communicate with stakeholders or the head of security.

7. Don't take any of your assets for granted.

Every asset is important and should not be taken for granted, just like any business can be targeted regardless of the size. Cybercriminals possess automated tools for scanning the web for vulnerabilities, and if they locate these in your infrastructures, they can take the chance to exploit your system and network.

CHAPTER THREE

How to Manage Administrative Privileges (IAM)

Identity and Access Management (IAM) must be part of the cybersecurity policies of an organization. It entails clarifying and managing the administrative rights and privileges that individual users within an organization can access and how these users are given or denied the privileges. The fundamental objective of IAM is ensuring a digital identity per user; once established, it must; throughout the users' access cycle, be maintained, improved, and supervised to enable a conducive working environment and mitigate abuses.1

Therefore, all organizations need an efficient IAM solution to protect themselves. However, the cost of a robust IAM solution might be too expensive for many small-to-medium enterprises; there are available free identity management tools for their use.

Although these tools should not be considered a replacement for a robust IAM solution, they have their capabilities that SMEs should harness because they lack adequate identity governance. In no particular order, these are some of the free and open-source tools:

Free Open-Source Tools for Identity Management

MidPoint

This tool combines identity management with identity governance. Developed by Evolveum as an open-source IAM tool, it is scalable, permitting organizations to have millions of users while offering diverse customization.

It has an auditing feature, evaluates the role catalog, and ensures compliance fulfillment. Its capacity for compliance assists small enterprises with the regulation of strict identity. While it works for every enterprise regardless of the size, its features are best suited for educational, financial, and governmental industries.

Apache Syncope

This platform is straightforward with its objective; 'managing digital identities in enterprise environments. It focuses mainly on providing identity storage, management of identity lifecycle, provisioning, password management, and capacities of access management capabilities. Also, it offers third party applications monitoring and security capabilities.

FusionIAM

Released under the BSD license, FusionIAM is a standard-compliant open-source IAM system. It features management of access control, LDAP directory, web services management, portal authentication, etc., available for IT business use to meet basic needs.

Soffid

Like other open-source IAM tools, it offers sole sign-on and identity management at the enterprise level. It aims to reduce costs of IAM support, assist with legal and auditing compliance, and facilitate the use of mobile devices via self-service portals; it provides roe management within the scope through set risk levels. Given identity governance and administration, Soffid offers reporting, workflow features, identity provisioning, and a unified directory.

Keycloak

This is unique among the open-source IAM tools considered here as it's designed to focus primarily on services and applications. It emphasizes third-party applications' identity security, which protects and assists a business in securing and monitoring third-party software with less coding. Keycloak offers usual user authentication and verification. Password policies, Standard protocols, unified management, etc., are some other features it offers.

OpenIAM

As one of the renowned open-source IAM tools, it has automated provisioning, sole sign-on, management of a single user or group, flexible verification, and more pertinent components of identity administration and governance. This tool reduces the business's operational cost and enhances identity audit in one control station, thereby helping enterprises attain their objectives at a reduced cost.

WSO2

This tool is one of the very few tools with Customer Identity and Access Management (CIAM) abilities. Should the business be into Customer Identity and Access Management, this tool promotes access with minimized friction to clients, management of modernized and customized preferences, and data gathering mainly for business intelligence.

This tool offers microservices and API security, provisioning, access control, identity connection, account management, and analytics.

Shibboleth Consortium

Being of the few globally known open-source IAM, this tool offers sole web sign-on, validation, and user data accumulation. When users request authentication, it enforces identity management policies, protecting the firm from external encroachment. It helps scale the growth of the firm beyond imagination. Also, it has both a metadata aggregator and a service provider as deployable business products.

Gluu

This open-source IAM tool synergizes cybersecurity platforms. The name captures its objective appropriately. It provides authentication of middleware for incoming users, directory integration, identity data storage, two-factor authentication, API access management, and approval server for the web.

Central Authentication Service (CAS)

Besides sole sign-on for the web, CAS offers an open-source Java server module, many integration capabilities, community documentation, support for multiple protocols, session and user authentication process, and implementation support.6

Some IAM solutions were not included in the tools above; they don't fit our standards for consideration. Though nearly all these free enterprise IAM solutions have paid services like implementation, installation, customization of developments, support, and cloud hosting, the fees are not costly.

Decision-makers in an enterprise are advised to slowly examine each of the IAM tools to determine which fits the requirement. You may have to try a few of them out, experiment with your team, compare the features offered, and the cost of each solution to know the best one available and suited for your enterprise.

Some benefits of using the IAM system:

The Identity and Access Management (IAM) has, among many others, the following benefits;

1.   Sole access to all the resources of the enterprise (SSO)

2.   Improved compacted management of privileges-having the right people in the right unit.

3.   Greater unified security

4.   Centralized auditing and logging

5.   Auditing, tracking, monitoring, and reporting users activities

6.   Enhanced compliance

7.   A single source of data source for Human Resources (HR)

8.   Easy management of privileges for employees

9.   Easy integration with the software and mobile applications of other firms

10.   Elimination of duplicity of accounts for enterprise systems

Despite the sources of documentation limited, open-source IAM tools make it easy to download applications and software and check how these suit the firm's needs and objectives with marginal efforts. Once the checks come with a positive outcome at a reduced cost, the saved cost can meet other needs. Small businesses have this leverage to protect themselves against data theft and grow to become larger   and   better.

CHAPTER FOUR

How to Establish Secure Configuration for Endpoints

The threat to the security landscape has changed as attackers have shifted their motive towards making money off holding data and devices hostage until the owner pays the ransom demanded. Technically, it is known as Ransomware attacks. To combat the threat, we delve into establishing secure configurations for endpoints and looking at free and open-source tools to help achieve it.

Endpoint security is the act of securing entry points or endpoints of end-user devices such as laptops, desktops, and mobile devices from being broken by malicious actors. Endpoint security systems protect endpoints in the cloud or on a network from cybersecurity threats. Endpoint security has evolved from traditional antivirus software to comprehensive protection from sophisticated malware and evolving zero-day threats.

Some of the **free and open-source tools** used to establish secure configuration for endpoints are;

TheHive Project

This is a platform for security incident responses for the general public. It was designed to assist CERTs, CSIRTs, and SOCs in enlisting faster security incident reports and substantiating practical strategies based on the various leeways observed in the information. It is an alliance platform that allows multiple investigators or analysts to work on the same thing simultaneously.

Features as live streaming, assignment of tasks, and online real-time information are available on this platform. It has a dynamic dashboard, features advanced filtering options, contains forensic and incident response and comprehensive cross-sectional reports.

SNORT

This robust open-source tool prevents intrusion by allowing users to recognize e-threats by systematically examining packet login and real-time network traffic. It is an easy to use device compatible with Centos, Fedora, FreeBSD, and Windows and is useful for investigations.

Some of its unique features are Multi-mode configuration (sniffer, packet logger, and Network Intrusion Detection System (NIDS)), Supports tunneling protocols: PPTP over GRE, MPLS, GRE, IP in IP, ERSPAN, and has multiple NIDS mode output options (Fast alert mode, Full alert mode, No alert mode, Unsock, Console, and CMG).

Open Source HIDS SECurity (OSSEC)

As an open-source and free software commonly addressed to small and medium scale businesses, large enterprises, and governmental agencies searching for server intrusion detection systems and solutions. It offers HIDS, HIPS, real-time Windows registry monitoring, log analysis, and other EDR features. OSSEC features Log-based Intrusion Detection (LIDS), Malware and Rootkit Detection abilities, File Integrity Monitoring (FIM), Quick and active responses, and System inventory.

OSSEC complies with many industry standards such as PCI-DSS and CIS and is compatible with Windows, Linux, OpenBSD, macOS, Solaris, and FreeBSD. It doesn't support any of the mobile platforms like Android or Mac OSX.

GRR Rapid Response

Licensed by Apache, this open-source incident response framework is used in virtual live forensics. The software performs minute forensic analyses on multiple endpoints. Its rapid response is compatible with most Linux, Microsoft Windows, and macOS X.

GRR, Rapid Response features are YARA Library support, Registry entries and files search and download, automation, increased scalability factor, and extensive monitoring abilities.

Ettercap Project

This is a cross-platform, open-source EDR tool that simulates ARP Poisoning and Man-in-the-Middle attacks on LAN. It boasts several security options like network traffic interception, network security auditing, active eavesdropping for the most mutual protocol, and protocol dissection. Compatible with Solaris, Linux, BSD, MacOS X, and Microsoft Windows, it features dual-mode (Wired or wireless), IP-based filtering, OS fingerprinting, and Plug-in support.

Nessus Vulnerability scanner

Nessus's lightweight and open-source software is a communication port-scanning tool useful for detecting system exposures – especially entry points susceptible to exploitation by malicious actors. Though it does not have full EDR abilities; nonetheless, it is efficient in identifying security breaches. Nessus is compatible with devices running Windows, Linux, and macOS.

Some of Nessus's features are Custom scripting and multiple plug-ins, In-depth vulnerability scanning, and Patching indicator. After deploying Nessus on the machine, it can perform up to 1,200 checks to identify system vulnerabilities.

Infection Monkey

This also is a free and open-source cybersecurity carriage assessment tool that simulates system breaches and Advanced Persistent Attacks (APTs). The software is for system admins who want to inquire about a company's security infrastructure, search for vulnerabilities, and investigators. Infection Monkey is compatible with macOS X, Microsoft Windows, and Linux.

Infection monkey features are running real-life infection scenarios and advanced detection abilities through methods like credential analysis, alerts on cross-segment traffic, and tunneling.

osQuery

Licensed by Apache device querying software, this open-source improves the visibility of connected devices. It uses simple SQL commands to produce complex 'relational data-models' by simplifying audits and investigations. It is useful for small and medium scale enterprises and is compatible with macOS, CentOS, Windows, FreeBSD, and Linux

Amongst many, some of osQuery's features are the Interactive querying console, useful host-monitoring daemon, modular codebase, file integrity monitoring, AWS logging, process auditing, YARA scanning, innovative log aggregations settings, anomaly detection, remote settings, and more.

Cuckoo Sandbox

This allows the end-user to analyze, isolate, and divide files demonstrating malicious behavior. It is compatible with Android, Microsoft Windows, Mac OS X, and Linux. It is a powerful file analyzer with useful network analysis and advanced memory. It analyzes network traffic before dumping by applying traffic encrypted with SSL or TLS.

Benefits of Secure Configuration for Endpoints

Some of the advantages are:

1.   It eliminates excessive and costly server downtime. Extreme demands on the server's resources from malware lead to down-time, which would curb customer-generated issues that result in customers being frustrated. The reputational damage this outage causes far outweigh any financial costs.

2.   It prevents issues even before they occur. Endpoint security software proactively observes the network, noticing the weak points where external devices can easily connect. They also assist in maintaining the health of the system.

3.   It helps to reduce costs, thereby saving money. The effect of any security issue costs time and money, mainly if

there is reputational damage. Spending a little more on providing a security solution saves time and money in the long run. Using the right security shifts the focus majorly to the daily tasks, which help keep business running more smoothly.

CHAPTER FIVE

How To Maintain, Monitor, and Analyze Audit Logs

E very device designed to secure IT networks comes with an in-built capacity to log events and act on the circumstances. These devices provide a record of past and present occurrences. It also offers protection against loopholes in application defenses and security perimeters by prompting you of threats so you can put up defensive measures before those threats take over your assets. You cannot put up defensive measures without real-time monitoring. You will only be left with the option of taking action after an application has been attacked.

It is crucial to monitor critical applications, endpoints housing sensitive or essential information, and other systems connected to vendors or third parties, or the internet. Every suspicious activity or critical issue should be added to the alert list and be correctly assessed and verified. Also, you will need to perform a risk assessment of every system and application to ascertain the level of audit, log review, as well as active monitoring that will be required. Here are some records you will need:

- Client or user IDs
- Terminal ID
- Key events such as date and time when logging in and out occurred.
- Networks and critical files accessed
- Modifications to system settings

- Use of network utilities
- Excepts and alarm triggered
- Activation of anti-malware and intrusion detection systems
- And other security-related events.

This information will bolster access control monitoring. It can also offer audit trails during the investigation of incidents.

So what are the free and open-source log management tools you can leverage without breaking the bank?

Event Log Consolidator

It sources Windows Event log from diverse data points and systems across your network and puts them in a repository. It then marks the trends and patterns across systems to enable you to observe persistent and dispersed security issues.

ManageEngine EventLog Analyzer

IT professionals utilize this administrative tool to source, manage, analyze, compare, and search through logged data from over 700 data sources by using both agent-based and agentless log collection tools. It allows you to import logs based if required. It clocks in 25,000 alerts per second with real-time threat detection. It can as well implement forensic analysis and minimize the impact of a security breach. The free version allows up to 5 log sources.

Kiwi Syslog Server

The free version is another useful log management tool. It obtains Syslog or traps from five systems and acts on alerting you and saving the information by utilizing filter rules.

Graylog Opensource

This tool utilizes a sidecar approach to obtain logs from your network. It has an easy-to-use user interface and provides visual log analysis functionality. It also permits the user to navigate through the massive volume of logs in no time using multi-core processors. You cannot audit in the free and open-source version. You will need to upgrade to do that.

GoAccess

This tool provides a real-time log analysis coupled with an intuitive log viewer, which you can access through a browser. You can also install it on a terminal. It is perfect for teams searching for a free and open-source web log analyzer to track HTTP statistics. GoAccess offers supports for logs from Apache, Nginx, and Amazon S3. You can monitor your web hosts' consumption rates and utilize a visual dashboard to generate a real-time view.

Conclusion

Covid-19 has seriously impacted business operations globally, and the effect will continue to be felt as the world struggles with the second wave of the virus. If you intend leveraging some of the tools mentioned in this book for on-the-budget cybersecurity, here some things you should include in your activities:

Keep yourself updated regularly:

Cyber threat is evolving, and the best means of developing resilience is to be conversant with emerging threats in the landscape. The next thing is to communicate with your team and alert your Security Operation Center or IT unit to proactively respond to any threat detected by those tools before it damages your critical assets.

Verify the people you collaborate with.

Most businesses invest in cybersecurity tools but underestimate insider threat. Attacks can be perpetrated by trusted associates, vendors, employees, and other stakeholders that possess easy access to your endpoint. Your best bet is to verify every access and ensure it is emanating from trusted persons. You can achieve this by establishing two-factor authentication.

Update the tools regularly

Since you are not spending much on tools, you need to commit considerable time and effort to download patches of the tools above tools. I have included their links in the reference and links section.

With these three tips, you have all it takes to achieve cybersecurity on a budget.

Reference and Links

Introduction

Gartner Says Global IT Spending to Grow 3.7% in 2020

https://www.gartner.com/en/newsroom/press-releases/2019-10-23-gartner-says-global-it-spending-to-grow-3point7-percent-in-2020.

Are You Getting Bang for Your Cybersecurity Budget Buck?

https://www.datacenterknowledge.com/security/are-you-getting-bang-your-cybersecurity-budget-buck#:~:text=A%20survey%20published%20late%20last,increase%20IT%20spending%20in%20general.

Chapter One

AssetTiger

https://www.myassettag.com/assettiger/

ManageEngine AssetExplorer

https://www.manageengine.com/products/asset-explorer/

Snipe-IT

https://snipeitapp.com/

Spice-works

https://www.spiceworks.com/

Lansweeper

https://www.lansweeper.com/

Microsoft Map Toolkits

https://www.microsoft.com/en-us/download/details.aspx?id=7826

Chapter Two

Nexpose Community

https://www.rapid7.com/products/nexpose/

OpenVAS

https://www.openvas.org/

Clair

https://coreos.com/clair/docs/latest/

Powerfuzzer

https://tools.kali.org/vulnerability-analysis/powerfuzzer#:~:text=Powerfuzzer%20is%20a%20highly%20automated,%2C%20modern%2C%20effective%20and%20working.

Moloch

https://github.com/arkime/arkime

Qualys Community Edition

https://www.qualys.com/community-edition/

Burp Suite Community Edition

https://portswigger.net/burp/communitydownload

Chapter Three

MidPoint

https://evolveum.com/midpoint/

Apache Syncope

https://syncope.apache.org/

FusionIAM

https://gitlab.ow2.org/fusioniam/fusioniam

Soffid

https://soffid.com/

Keycloak

https://www.keycloak.org/

OpenIAM

https://www.openiam.com/

WSO2

https://wso2.com/identity-and-access-management/

Shibboleth Consortium

https://www.shibboleth.net/

Gluu

https://www.gluu.org/

Central Authentication Service (CAS)

https://iam.uconn.edu/cas/

Chapter Four

The Hive Project

https://thehive-project.org/

SNORT

https://www.snort.org/

OSSEC

https://www.ossec.net/

GRR

https://grr-doc.readthedocs.io/en/v3.2.1/what-is-grr.html#:~:text=GRR%20Rapid%20Response%20is%20an,attacks%20and%20perform%20analysis%20remotely.

ETTERCAP

https://www.ettercap-project.org/

NESSUS

https://www.tenable.com/products/nessus

INFECTION MONKEY

https://www.guardicore.com/infectionmonkey/

osQuery

https://osquery.io/

Cuckoo Sandbox

https://cuckoosandbox.org/

Chapter Five

Event Log Consolidator

https://www.solarwinds.com/free-tools/event-log-consolidator

ManageEngine EventLog Analyzer

https://www.manageengine.com/products/eventlog/download-free.html

Kiwi Syslog Server

https://www.kiwisyslog.com/free-tools/kiwi-free-syslog-server

Graylog Opensource

https://www.graylog.org/downloads-2

GoAccess

https://goaccess.io/